HEART SONGS

POEMS

Kraftgriots

Also in the series (POETRY)

HEART SONGS

POEMS

Akachi Adimora-Ezeigbo

kraftgriots

Published by

Kraft Books Limited
6A Polytechnic Road, Sango, Ibadan
Box 22084, University of Ibadan Post Office
Ibadan, Oyo State, Nigeria
℃ +234 (2) 7523177, 0803 348 2474, 0805 129 1191
E-mail: kraftbooks@yahoo.com

First published 2009

ISBN 000–000–0000–0–0

= KRAFTGRIOTS =
(A literary imprint of Kraft Books Limited)

First printing, February 2009

Dedication

To
Dr T.C. Nwosu
For believing that I'd get there
And for being there for me

Acknowledgements

Acknowledgements are due to Aboki Publishers, Makurdi, who first published "Farewell Great Compatriot" under the title "Farewell" and "Ode to the Successful Woman Writer" in the volume, *Five Hundred Nigerian Poets* (2005), edited by Jerry Agada.

I am grateful to Royal Holloway, University of London, for inviting me as A Visiting Research Fellow in 2006/2007 academic year, thus providing the opportunity and enablement that gave birth to this collection.

Many thanks to the following people for their support in the United Kingdom: Professors Elleke Boehmer, Robert Hampson, Stephanie Newell and Ms Patricia Bryden.

Preface

I was tempted to write an introduction to these poems, but then as a disciple of Reader Response Theory, I decided to ignore the temptation, not only because the poems are easily accessible to a poetry connoisseur but also because I believe that a poetry collection ought not to be inflicted with an author's or a critic's interpretation but left as it really is, virginal, pure and provocative, to be plumbed and savoured by the reader who comes to it as a lover, expecting to be charmed, entertained, educated and completely satisfied.

I was invited to Royal Holloway University of London as a Research Fellow for the purpose of researching and writing fiction, but I found myself consorting with poetry. Poetry chose me; I did not choose poetry. However, I capitulated. Once I was ensconced in *his* warm embrace, I fell deeply in love. In this collection are recorded the conversations, the dialogue we had and the precious moments we shared. Make of this what you will; it is completely up to you, the reader.

It is a marvel that I have at last come up with a poetry collection, I who was said to be trapped in the cavernous cave of fiction. But, the truth is I have flirted with poetry since I was eighteen, but never took the affair seriously until 2006 when I began to write profusely, consistently and meditatively at Royal Holloway University of London. Having made this first attempt at publishing my poems in a collection, I display them to the gaze of my 'fans', 'critics' and friends, hoping that I would not be considered immodest when I declare that *ahia oma na-ere onwe ya* – a good product sells itself.

This potpourri of poems inspired by disparate themes and other sundry events and experiences in three continents–Africa, Europe and North America–is a signifier of our globalized reality today. Before you, then, is a well-garnished poetic dish meant to warm and enliven the cold dark days spurned by our chilling climes that compel you oftentimes to question the worth of existence in this vale of tears, our world.

The songs of a heart
*un*manacled
freed at last
from roaming
the subterranean passages
in a dungeon of silence
given a voice
in a season of retrieval
and clear-sightedness.

Akachi Adimora-Ezeigbo, Lagos, 2009

Contents

Satirical Tunes

Ram syndrome
(To victims of naked power)

from the Ancients
wise words:
he who consumes
the testicles of a ram
owes *ibi* a debt–
scrotum disease;
penis pilfering
prohibited:
penalty?
ram albatross
early symptom:
loss of favour
and patronage
the risk is all yours
to your peril
a scourge.

the rhythm of
Igba dance
once tasted
disqualifies
a performer from
digging
Odogwu dance

dance of the basket
separates chaff from grain
one does not
face two directions
simultaneously
you cannot be

tortoise
as well as
turtle:
ask former Russian muscle man
Alexander Litvinenko
bold defection
bought him
one way ticket
to the land of no return

fly does not
play near spider's web:
ask Russian gadfly
Anna Politkovskaya

grasshopper keeps
some distance
when it hears
the raucous music
of *okpoko* bird:
ask Dele Giwa
ask also race victim
Amadou Diallo

antelope does not leap
into lion's den:
ask Ken Saro-Wiwa

lizard does not
visit a hedge
where cat
takes a nap:
ask Bola Ige
Who does not know
that jackal does not

forgive an affront?
ask freedom choirmaster
Moshood Abiola
and his faithful consort to
martyrdom: Kudirat;
ask also that colourful
politician, Chuba Okadigbo

it has not always been
like this
the end is different
from the beginning
the end
justifies the outcome
the means
justifies the beginning

when ally acts
as accuser
when adviser becomes
critic
murky murder
mounts by the minute
clouds each concern
promotes unaccountable
uncontrollable
police state
in the guise of
democracy–
demon-crazy–
spearheading
relentless attacks
on individual liberty
on genuine freedom

Homeless

spied upon
derided
verbally attacked
shot dagger looks–
if looks could kill
you'd be dead
long ago–
many times over

Brother, *haba*!
scum of metropolis
impaled on asphalt

wandering far from home
where a home awaits
the homeless

waif of highways
skunk emitting stinking secretion
skulking in corners
slime of slippery streets
skim-milk bereft of cream
your situation is quite grim
what's the matter
with your grey matter?

who are you?
sewage rat
foraging in bins
hunger gnaws your guts
because you lost your guts
hole in your hat
hate in your heart
dirty nails
adorn feet with cracked heels

and callused hands with nine fingers
the tenth mince meat for a watchdog

some sight!
cold calcified limbs
face pinched
graying hair
victim of premature ageing
or inclement weather
whipping winter winds
wailing after you
in hot pursuit
down alleys
blown to the Underground
you hobble along
searching for warmth
as rare as hair
on a monkey's buttocks

what are you?
stray dog
or illegal immigrant?
Britons empathize with
the former, not the latter
living on the street
robs you of your humanity
you litter the corner
with your bulky body
clothed in so many rags
caked by filth
matted hair
poor imitation dreadlock
runny nose
flaring nostrils
and ravine mouth
belching fumes
of harmless smoke
as you stagger along

looking for cast-offs
and leftovers
that often do not exist

just think of it:
most Britons prefer
stray dogs to
stray humans
living off the street–
homeless!

most Londoners think
doling money to beggars
causes more harm than good
smug in this belief
presages atrophy of conscience

go home, homeless
turn your trash to cash;
but if you fail
better to die
buried in
warm soil
watched over by
 Sun
  &
 Moon
  &
 Stars
in the land of
your birth
than frozen stiff
in a hostile hole

The 'ism' of race

I travelled
    to a country
        that was not
            my own
I was
    a stranger
        in town;
            like a chicken
                in a strange place
                I stood
                    on one leg.

Wouldn't look
    people in the eye
        fearing they'd
            frown

Sneer at
    recoil from
        despise
            hate
            ME
                and make
                    ME feel unwanted

        Time-rooted
        Hard-grounded
        City-wise
        I survived

I'm surviving

    now I live here
        chills and frowns
            exclusions
                notwithstanding

Call ME
Atakata agbuo+ –
    This is my new name

        (+ Great survivor)

Fallen tyrant

A court guard chewed gum and laughed
Blew bubble and flicked his tongue like a lizard
Mocking the fallen tyrant with shaky legs
Power pass power
Two leopards overpowered a rampaging hyena
Strong man with bronze feet, broken shield
Crumbling massive structure
Toppled images and fractured rocks
Crashing down the mountain
Death strewn weeds along the pathway
In the midst of unspeakable carnage
Nemesis came, calling

Return journey
Is shorter than outward journey
Ask those who plied the route before–
Adolf Hitler, Idi Amin, Mobutu, Pinochet–
Is there a sting without antidote?
Is there a tree that can populate a forest?
Those who thrive by sword
Will not escape its sharp-edged justice

The downfall of the hyena was predictable–
It shone hard enough for the blind to see
Rang loud enough for the deaf to hear
It was putrid enough for mucus-blocked nose
To smell its rottenness kilometers away–
Its birth pangs provoked acts

Of internal and external aggression
Rooted in invasions, massacres and genocide*
Would all tyrants be damned
Before their flood drowns everything in sight?

---

* It was reported that Saddam Hussein invaded Iran in 1980 and Kuwait in 1990. He said to have massacred, in 1982, about 150 Shia Muslims in Dujai–revenge killing it was called. In 1988, he was alleged to have murdered 50,000 Kurds and soon after the Gulf War killed 5,000 civilians in the Kurdish town of Halabja.

Lootocracy

Wisdom twisted
Black signifies white
White turns black
Shroud of reason

Season of deceit
Disease of the mind
O dementia!
Schizophrenia
The more you look, the less you see
The more you know, the less you understand
Time-tested slogans–
Knowledge is power
Time is money
Tempus fugit–
Politicians dance naked
Fully clothed, cap in hand
Standing before His Excellency
Salaaming. In obeisance to the ace marksman
Whose shot never misses target
Whose goods never lack markets
Disciple of Oscar Wilde's aphorism:
'Moderation is a fatal thing.
Nothing succeeds like excess.'
The clowns in a game of greed
Adopt this as their creed
Uproot caution
Enthrone indiscretion
The fruits long have ripened
The harvest well underway
In the orchard of lootocracy

Ubiquitous parasites
Eyeing the bursting treasury
Looting national treasures
For personal pleasures

Victims of our wars

(For war victims in africa and other theatres of war: Past & present)

How many war mongers pause to think
Of the tragedy their actions spawn
Like a pond full of countless tadpoles?–
Fields devastated by locust invasions
Trees stripped of their greens
Soil rendered infertile and sterile
Cities pillaged by modern-day pirates
Reduced to rubble by weapons of mass destruction
Communities decimated and displaced
Countries depopulated and dehydrated

How many warlords worry about the bloodbath
Their endless battles cause in so-called war zones
Like a storm accompanying a hurricane?–
Pause, O Hawks of war and spare a thought:
Feel compassion, deep inside you for
Women who lost their children
Babies without breasts to suck
Multitudes without homes to return to
Millions of women defiled, violated

Orphans left in limbo, rootless
Thousands of victims who lost their minds to grief

Peace let the world know
Let anger cease, love flow like a river
To cleanse every soul of war pollution
There will be time to reflect on our humanity
As nations gather to celebrate life not death

Praise Songs: Celebating Lives

Uhamiri's haven

Woman of the Lake
Relic of the past, you linger in our memory
You who held sway in days gone by
Powerful deity, beautiful goddess
Your watery presence was

Acknowledged by locals and visitors
Your priests and priestesses revered
You, kept alive your rituals and mores
But Flora it was who spread your fame
Made your name a household word
In huts and palaces throughout the globe
Propelled you into the embrace of the literati
Immortalized you in her numerous works–
Gems that adorn our literary hall of fame

That fame it was drew us to your kingdom
Ugwuta Lake to view; the home of Ogbeide
Your other lesser known name. We were
On excursion. Owerri our first port of call
After our idyllic stay at Concorde Hotel
We arrived Ugwuta, made haste to the Lake

O Goddess, our eyes lit up to behold your zone
Sunshine courted you, swooned upon you
Intoxicated by your depth, your wide girth
Your calm sweetness held him captive
As reward for your hospitality, your invitation
He shone on you till you bathed in light
Your beauty exploding in scintillation
Birthing a galaxy of stars on water
There stood we, thirty of us–

Wives of surveyors, our consorts
Escorting them to their annual ritual of meetings—
Striking out on our own to bond with you
Who know no consort and reared no offspring
Yet you are goddess of love, beauty and fertility
Mothering and nurturing writers and critics
Besides the people of your land

Live on, then, in your legendary palatial rooms
Splendid Kingdom of water and fishes half-human
Let the gritty politics of oil scourge surrounding lands—
A daughter of Delta though you may claim—
It will not mar your beauty or rob you of people
Who throng your zone as tourists and guests
Attracting wealth that no controversy defiles

Gem for all seasons

(For prof. Chinyere okunna, commissioner of information,
anambra state)

Child of my mother
I call you by day
and by night
in dreams. Presences
no tardiness invite.

Able
capable
at beck and call
moments, hours
unfailing.

Rare gem
shrewd shoot
sprouting in the
cultured clan of
the Great-King.

One among
descendants
of kings
mothered by a
princess greater
than Queen of Sheba.

She gave you birth
suckled you with
her life-giving sap
exhaled. *Ayayaya!*

carbon copy
yet finer.

Wise at dawn
time's favourite child
born to lead
eagle feather unrivalled
inine opokonja nwa.

Youthful
beautiful
woman to the core
sharp machete
that cuts *achara*
your headdress firm
on your rich head.

Rossetti knew well
sisterhood to warble
I might not buy
from Goblin Market
but know fully well
more you would risk–
sacrifice more striking
to bail a sister.

The elements are
no deterrent to
your calculated haste
into troubled waters
deep plunge
to salvage!

Savage determination

your example
far out-shines
Lizzy's for her
beloved Jane.

Ada eji eje mba!
vanguard voice of women
mass communicators.

Calabash fit for heroes
your wine vessel shall be
health to your household
life for your labours.

Power to your pen
as you communicate
with the world
about your people
for your people

Social worker

Rare as oyster in River Niger
Jewel of a woman
O Sensitive social worker
Where is that oasis in the desert
Of our arid and denuded land?
A beacon on a hill-top
A flashing light in life's lighthouse
Ray of hope: a drop of golden sun
Let it be a boon
Sent from the God of mercy
Rare creature
Garlanded with eagle feather–
Okpu otu-ugo:*
Understanding people
Is your forte
Empathizing
Learning to hold

Not letting go
Filament of gestures
Incandescent wire of feelings
Possessing the secret of faith
And the triumvirate:
Trust
Truth
Tenderness

Pain extinguisher
Pathway to recovery
Love and friendship ignite
Psychic comprehension
Of the feel, taste and need

Of every client
Every patient
People can be
Fascinating
Mystifying
Mortifying
Terrifying
Downright nasty
Ungrateful
But, also
Rewarding
Loving
Cool
Cute.
You accept them as they come
Social work is work with people
Intriguing in its simplicity
And complexity
Aha! Social workers wanted
But, as professional as they come
You top the list.

(* Symbol of recognition.)

Music evergreen

For me Rain King is still tops
among revered reggae maestros
music at its best I'd say,
in the tradition of Bob's
West Indian heavily
syncopated rock music.
Majek for me any day
decades after his wonder
hit that really brought down
the rain for me,
listening to the rhythm
I swing high as I do
when watching a regatta,
it's no fake! Better than
the original from calypso land

let's tell our youths
to excel in creative impulses
and produce like masterpieces,
let's export music not cocaine
let us market talent not fraud

Njakiri: Songs in Pidgin

Cultism

I dey happy say I no be young man again
As I don reach de age of *di-okpa*
Wisdom don give me plenty grey hair sef
I happy well though I worry for today youths
Dem no do well at all; dem offense too much

Yes, youth go act like youth, we know
But too much of everyting bad
Small mistake no go do harm
To young people, instead dem learn lesson

But dis secret cult no be mistake
Na real crime, proper murder
As dem cultist just dey butcher people
Like dem be Fulani cattle, abi Bamenda goat

Dem say dem papa na big men for de country
Kickin dem don spoil with plenty money
Dis people tink say money be everyting
Dem tink say dem money can buy anyting
Name your price. Everyting get him price

Like joke, like joke, de pickin dey drug
Dem smoke grass–igbo, wee wee
Kaikai dem drink like water sef
Womanize pass sojaman and sailor

School dem no wan go again
Lecturers dey chop money for nothing
De youths no wan stay for classroom
If I be de President of dis country

I go prosecute every cultist and him papa
If him kill somebody, him and him papa go die
If na manslaughter, na life sentence dem go get
Yes, *ke*. If bird dey fly, dey fly witout perching
Na so hunter go dey shoot witout aiming

Nudity

Chei, which kind madness
Catch women for present time?

Abi na my eye only dey see am?
De ting dey ground since new millennium

But, every year na him de ting get worse
Like fire we catch dry forest for Harmattan

From Lagos to Sokoto, you go see am
From Maiduguri to Port Harcourt

Why everybody no talk, just dey look
Like *mumu* wey just wake from sleep

Dem call am show belly, show bobby
Tits as tempter; boobs as booby trap

You enter school, you go see am plenty
You wakka go church, na dere de ting *bokwu*

Topless is to operation bare your breasts as
Striptease is sequel to show your pubic region

I mean to say one day dem fit go stark naked
If government do noting to stop dis madness

De one wey vex me be say old woman dey do
Some go oyinbo country for lift up dem boobs

I wan make government arrest woman
Wey commot for house naked or half naked

Peraps some of una vex with me, dey tink
Government no be 'moral police'

Even so, enough be enough. Dis nakedness
I say i don do! I don talk my own

If daughter dey drown, mama dey drown
Na who go save de one and de oder?

Dat na de question I wan leave for dem
All de women of we country go answer am

Madonna and baby david

Since my mama born me
I never see dis kain ting
One oyinbo woman come from
Far away America go Malawi–
Oyinbo call am 'poverty stricken country'–
De woman name be Madonna, big celebrity
Him talk say one Jewish spiritual club
Tell am say make him go do goody goody
Na him i come Malawi give plenty money
For orphanage, adopt one pikin from de place

I vex plenty as de pikin papa happy well well
Foolish man give him pikin away like gift
Fine man-pikin; him name be David
I hear say Madonna give million dollar
To orphanage and hospital for Malawi
Including promise of investment and trade
Malawi people dey dance, government happy

I dey cry for Baby David, for him papa
For Malawi, for Africa, for Black man
Na wetin happen to we make we beggars like dis
We swim for poverty, in spite of we resources
We hungry pass people of de whole world
We sick pass everybody: kwashiorkor, HIV/AIDS
Every flying disease or problem go visit Africa

Make I ask one question sef
Dis Madonna: na wetin she be
Manipulator or mother?
De woman don carry David go America
No be so him people carry black people

Go work for plantation as slaves
Today, some still carry we women go Italy
To do *ashawo* work with man or dog
Dem call am human trafficking
Slave trade wey get new face

Na wetin wrong with Africa sef?
Abi, black man no get sense?
Na we de first kill we self
Before outside people finish we
Look de kain leaders we get sef
See as we follow dem like *ode, mumu*
Dem lead we for bush, we follow
Like person wey blind
All we money don enter dem pocket
We no even worry or ask question

I dey pray for Baby David and
De next Malawi pikin Madonna adopt
Wetin dem go be when dem grow up?
Make dem no become misfits for America
Make dem no carry gun or smoke *wee wee*
Make dem remember dem root, dem people
Money good, but money no be everyting
Money no fit buy love, identity, peace of mind
Na true word I talk

Monkey dey work, baboon dey chop

Me I no go do factory work again, *lai lai*
Na igedu work be dat, suffer man work

Big oga dey for office, suffer man dey
Factory de kill himself with work

Seven o'clock for morning i don come
Na dere him go tanda sote seven nack

Some dey do overtime sef, Saturday and Sunday
Public holiday dem work sote dem tire

Minimum wage dem get year by year, no increment
But oga him money dey grow like tree for bank

Na so I work for slippers factory for ten years
My body tire, come old: khaki no be leather

Na proper victim we be, men and women
Money no cover food, housing and school fees

Even sef we no fit buy better cloth to wear
Money no do for pay hospital bill

Small ting you go do, dem fire you
I no fit count de number of people dem sack

Na so so risk we dey take; life no safe at all
Why because de owner lock him door–

Dis door dem call am 'emergency exit'
Dem make am to be open all de time

Oga dem fear worker go thief dem slippers
And smuggle am commot, pass back gate

Na him one day God save me; I no go work
We factory catch fire, kill plenty workers

I hear say workers dey shout, dey shout
Nobody open door; fire roast dem like yam

Na him make me say I no fit work for factory
Again, even if you double money ten times!

Tornado jam london

My brodda, I don see someting
Wey make me fear plenty for de world
But nothing shock me like de tornado
Wey tear London like old rag

I go London visit my father him brother son
Na my first visit be dat; I dey happy well well
I don run away from we country headache
Na better place I dey now: na so I tink for mind

Na North London I dey, for Kensel Rise
I dey look fine house, fine road, better bus
Danfo no dey dere; Molue sef I no see
I no see gutter at all, everyting dey underground
I no forget de day: Thursday, December 8, 2006,
Day of tornado be dat; day of Armageddon
Fire and brimstone. Hell don enter de world
I dey quake with fear, I dey tink terrorist bomb London

My kinsman run commot for house; I follow *gbam*
Kata kiti, kata kiti, Na run be dat
We reach front door; my leg no move again
De ting I see blow my mind; I just tanda dere
I dey wonder if I dey dream, if my mind dey sick

Dis tornado behave like mad man. Na waa!
De wind break wall, pull off roof and tile
Smash window, scatter glass for ground
I shout, come fall down, shaking like leaf
Chei, my eye see someting

As I look de wicked wind uproot plenty tree
Blow dem across road; one fall on top of car
Chei, na wetin be dis? Wind dey shift car
Across street, fling brick and bin into de air

Someting hit me *gbam* for head; na roof tile
And I hear *girigidi* as one wall fall for we house
Plenty ting dey fly for air, like acrobat dancer
I see darkness cover everyting for few second

Small time de tornado pass: I surprise well well
Na short time, but plenty damage dey every corner
Dem talk say one hundred and fifty house damage
And de speed of de wind reach 210 kph

Medical people look my head, give am First Aid
Dem carry we go one emergency centre, in a church
We sleep for dis place with other displaced persons
I dey tink which kain bad luck be dis wey follow me

But as I dey tink, my mind tell me say hope dey
Dis one na natural tornado; oyinbo people fight am
Dem go bring money repair all de damage
But for we country, we get artificial tornado

Na de politician dey make tornado every time
Dem thug carry gun, rock, club to scatter everyting
Like de one wey happen for Awka and Odi
Yea, we own na man-made tornado

As I dey tink, water dey commot for my eye
I dey sorry for we country;
I dey sorry for myself.

Cancer

Wich kain disease
Be dis one wey fit
Kill person like chicken?
If na say i don catch you
Na die be dat. No cure.

I dey wonder
For dis cancer sef
No part of body
Dey free from attack
When i enter body
Katakata don come
Na so i go bulldoze
Right, left and centre.

Woman bobby no escape
Kidney dey for danger
Liver *nko*? Lung nko?
No respect for dem, *gbam*!

Na so i fight blood, skin
And nose, mouth and eye
Cancer no get mercy at all.

Even sef, inside body no safe
Woman body dey sweet cancer pass
Cervix be 'im house; ovary no escape sef
Bowel–*abi* colon na rectum
Prostrate *nko*?–
Dem say na biggest cancer for man
Like breast cancer for woman

I dey fear dis prostate cancer too much
Wey don finish black man *pata pata*

Wetin man go do sef?
If cancer *bokwu* everywhere
How person go fit escape am?

Suffer-head immigrant

Countryman, my eye see *alu*
De time I visit my uncle pikin
For oyinbo country

I come see plenty immigrant
Dem flood de place like water
Dem full de place like locust
Migrant worker dem be.

Even sef, I dey hungry
Make me tanda dere begin work
Sote I see as dem suffer
For oyinbo man hand.

Plenty plenty exploitation
Spite of dem big qualification
Upon de fact many be graduate
Dem get small money pass
Son-of-de-soil wey no go school.

Na small small right dem get
Plus dangerous working condition
Dem money na one pound per hour
Upon all de plenty work dem do
For oyinbo; all de profit for economy
For public service, for national life

Old-boy, listen, make I tell you
I see plenty white people
Dey do this sufferhead work
Some from Poland, Portugal, Romania
Plenty from Pakistan and India sef

Filipino dey; some from Brazil and Croatia.

Black man and woman dey plenty
Some get big certificate, big degree:
Masters, doctor, professor sef
Plenty get employment far below
Dem skill level. My mouth open like cave
As shock catch me; I see one accountant
Wey be cleaner for hospital
One doctor be waiter for restaurant
Professor dey wash Tube Station
Another be security guard for one office

I dey wonder: wetin oyinbo man de do?
Dem wan bring back Charles Dickens time?
No be dis kain exploitation make de man
Write plenty book 'bout worker suffer-head
Plus how life be for poor people?

As shock leave me, I begin vex no be small
Africa no see doctor, teacher no dey
Better hospital, road, house no dey
Our people come here do *igedu* work.

I dey curse African leader dem
Wey spoil country, make people run away
To oyinbo country where need no dey for dem
Dem do de kain work oyinbo man no gree do
Sweating for low-skilled job
De kain work dem no fit do for Africa!

As man live na so man die

As man live
Na so man die
>Big man, small man
>Death dey wait for am

Even sef you get power
Pass everybody

>Or you get money plenty
>Na so you go answer
>Death call one day

De ting you do go kill you
De life you live go finish you

I go choose my work well
I no go do just any work

>I no do pilot job *lai lai*
>One day pilot go die for crash

Driver work no be for me
One day moto go kill am
>Mine work nko? No, no, no
>One day mine go fall on top of miner

Ashawo work? Sometime life sweet am
But one day, one crazy customer go kill am
If not, one kain disease finish am
Like HIV/AIDS or VD

Since my Mama born me
Even now I be grown man
I see say people die as dem live
Na dis make me begin dey tink

    I wan be Pastor or Imman
    Make I work for God

If I die for dis work, no matter
Na Paradise me dey go
To chop life bellyful

Na so life be

For we country
Person different different
De ting wey wory one person
No be im worry anodder person

But, I tink i better make person
Take sense dey live im life
As life no be de same for everybody.

Dis ship dem call marriage
Some people wan run comot
Dem ship don hit rock
Some dey struggle make dem enter
        Na so life be.

You wan go *obodo* oyinbo?
You tink life be sugar
For oyinbo dem country?
You no know
Person wey wan enter battle
Go prepare well well
For battle na call of death?
        Na so life be.

Person wey do 419 business
One day one day, dem catch am
Person wey dance *usurugada*
Must know *usurugada* dance
Be dance for dead people
        Na so life be.

Some woman tink na sense be dat:
De only ting dey im mind na cloth;
How to buy plenty gold trinket
Plus plenty designer shoe
Including handbag and headtie dem
Na only money talk she sabi
Na dat go make life better?
Na dat go bring peace of mind?
All dat fit bring joy?
  Na so life be.

Old boy, dat your teenage pikin
You give am big moto to drive
All corner of town de moto reach
When de pikin reach thirty years
Na trailer i go drive?
  Na so life be.

Make I tell you:
We no grateful *lai lai*
For de ting God give we
For dis we country.
When I go oyinbo country
I come know cold dey kill
Na for dat place I sabi
Say heat na proper medicine
Hot water na cure for sickness
  Na so life be.

Listen to me well well
Make you dey happy, you hear?
No worry about anything
Enjoy de ting you get for dis life
Yes, enjoy am, with good sense
  Na so life be.

Sex machine

Chei, chei, chei!
God forbid bad ting
Some people dey annoy me
De ting dem do no good
     How I no go talk?

    King Utunko
You spoil people dem pikin
Your own dey for cover
You guard dem like treasure
But de woman you spoil no be few
     One day, your offense go catch you

    Mark my word
De ting you give
Na him you go receive
You be sex machine
Wey dey shine
You no dey tire?
     Soon you go backfire

    Tufiakwa!
You just dey work
As if na Viagra dey work
You tanda for house of pleasure
     Dashing away your treasure.

    End of talk:
A beg, reduce your pace
Give wisdom some space
In your womanizing mind.

Gendered Musings

Chicken gizzard

Gizzard culture
Guarded ritual
of ancient culture
bizarre cult
'O Woman
this meat is taboo to you'–
his vulgar spite-coated voice
assaults her long-suffering ears
chastised by a din of dos and don'ts–
dressed in any form:
fresh, dripping blood, frozen, stiff like rod
steamed, greased, cooked
in a griddle or over a gridiron
the tradition is secure, sure
it's no delicacy or food for your kind
as our ancestors decreed
so it will remain times to come
grilled or roasted
fried or barbecued
the verdict irreversible
for you and all like you

Grim faced, she stares aghast
eyes scavenging for victims' carrion
mind excavating centuries of oppression
unnumbered seasons of suppression
unprovoked, to say the least
gizzard monopoly is but one
of several inhuman games, acts
of *male*volent posturing

Grimace involuntary her visage assails

a grin intervenes. Sheepishly
then raw rage charging forward
teeth grinding, she grabs the gizzard
wrenching with might, freeing it
from the bloody carcass
of the just-slaughtered supper chicken

Plunk! With passion, into the bin
She flings it, eyes fuming, nose flaring
'Yah! There goes your grisly gizzard!
And your cruel custom as well!'

African male lizard

With my hammer head
wielded with force of gravity
I subdue all and sundry–
the elements to my will
my harem to my charm
freely, oh, freely I roam
scaling walls, hills and cliffs
descending with ease
into valleys and vaults
innumerable treasures
at my beck and call
copulating with all my charges
consorting with old and young
never being challenged
by any dead or alive
ranging from moss to rock
creeping into craters and crevices
over brambles and branches
come rain come shine
undeterred, unmolested
navigating boulders
and bottlenecks
food for my privileged stomach
leftovers for the underprivileged *other*
and sand for the deprived many
freedom is sweet
but sweeter in solitary enjoyment
at the expense of the *other*
living in bondage

Power to the women

'Women empowered'
Is millions helped
In the home
At work
Equity should be
The game
This must be
The maxim
In Africa,
Everywhere.

Empowering women
Is key to improvement:
For women's lives
For children's lives.

Nourishment
        is to nutrition
As healing
        is to health
As enlightenment
        is to education

Key role players
Women in family
      Nutrition
          Health
              Education.

Gender equality
Marches hand in hand

With children's well-being
Produces prosperity and
Harmony in homes
Welcoming it.

Haiku melody

1. Month of December
    Hail! Hallowed by rare virgin birth
    Harmattan dust bathed

2. Madness in the sea
    clash of waters foaming white
    like sweet fresh palm wine

3. A tingle, a thrust
    heart thumping wanting to burst
    reaping ecstasy

4. Winter air brittle
    I can break it with fingers
    like slender dry twigs

5. Your weird lack of trust
    Stifles, feeds fat on my fear
    vile immolation

Love Songs

Separation

I don't pretend to be
The other leg of your compass
Separation severs touch
Absence absorbs images
Absolves vows

I miss you so, pining for you
If only I could be sure
Your heart beats a little bit for me
When thoughts of me rise
In the chamber of your mind

Sealed tongues

Different tongues we speak
Born in different wards and clans
Clannishness we abhor
Welcome, O binding bond of love
That binds our hearts
Beating each for each. Sweet melody
Sealing our two tongues into one

Blessing in disguise

Day dawned, drab
on the morning you left
grief gripped me for months
I cowered indoors
mourning your loss.

Return of sunshine
signalled new beginnings
joy unfurled again like foliage
in Ozara forest of springs
the day my true love appeared
intuition assured me he'd come to stay.

Lost love

Cacophony of sounds
Screeching of tyres
Wails, suppressed cry
High-speed crash
Car high-powered
Ploughed into a lamp-post
Purloined my angel
Soulmate rare
Kindred spirit spirited away
Before his prime

He was light and sight
Different from his kind
Special. Unique
Brilliant mind, hatching humour
Fixing fun, charting our chats
Pure joy. A guardian angel
Irreplaceable
I adored him and always will
With him happiness was tangible
To be reaped for good reason

I am myself still–in appearance only
Mind and heart broken, splintered
Gone forever. I will never love again

To the nunnery I'll retire

Baby mine

Lusty screams
Announced your birth
O birth rites, passage raw and rough
Birth pangs! Agony indescribable
Undaunted, you shooting out
Like a star
Following moments of last
Communion with ancestors
And the beginning of
Dialogue with the living
You survived transition stage

Now I have you to myself
To hold and cuddle
Flesh of my flesh
Bone of my bone
You are mine and mine alone

Under the oilbean tree

Time of oilbean
Cracking of pods
Exploding to germinate
The cycle of reproduction
In the middle of harmattan
Dusty air ripe with dryness
Cracking pods
Blistering lips
A memorial
Of our first tryst
    Under the oilbean tree.

Remember the nectar
Distilled from oilbean blossoms,
Sweet as our love,
Syrupy, oozing
Like a nursing mother's milk
Fills our mouths
As we feel each other
Filling our hearts
    Under the oilbean tree.

Mother waiting
Waiting for me
Before setting out
For *ozuru* market
Which thrived at dusk
Oil lamps glittering
Shining here, there
Everywhere
For the night traders
    Under the oilbean tree.

You were ever gentle
Patient as a dove
Invoking memories
Of a past life
I could not fathom
Or recall
For the life of me
But sensed I lived
With you
Or someone like you
        Under the oilbean tree.

The vow I made that day
Would renew itself
As days passed
I loved you
Always did
From the day
You first kissed me
        Under the oilbean tree.

Remember how we laughed
Plumbing our feeling
Its depth astonishing
Stirring our empathy
A pot of healing herbs
Ours to taste, savour
        Under the oilbean tree.

As late oilbean pods
Exploded with glee
To herald
Love that would grow and grow
That would not let us go
But must feed our flame
        Under the oilbean tree.

Kpawaram!
Kpawaram!
Kpawaram!
The explosions
That proclaimed
And sealed our love
        Under the oilbean tree.

Love feast

Come, the one
who rules my heart,
and my thoughts
sing a serenade
love's ultimate food
and I will dance
like a butterfly
flutter around you
a fresh breeze to fan
and cool your sweaty brow

Render a lullaby of love
and send my goddess eyes
to immortal sleep
let me wake to eternity
lying next to you
as we clutch our dream bodies
anointed with precious oil
nourished with music

Passion

Passion
    Is
       A storm
          Only two
             Can
               Ride
    Heights
    Unknown
    Depths
    Unfathomed
Level ground
Shunned
They come
Afterwards
    Calm after
    Supine
    Sated
    Drop down
Like a flea
Gorged
With blood
Oblivion

A lover waiting

The door is shut
but not locked
unwise to leave it open
someone else could enter
unwanted.

The waiting is long.
What's the matter?
Delay unforeseen
mysterious
instructions had been clear.
Fear nibbles
heart's string
snap?
Mercy!
Back to window–
one in a multitude
a ghostly figure
behind curtains
worry-worn
eyes reach out, rove
focus
tabled burdened
clammy, cold
mess of a meal
flaccid like
thawed frozen fish.

In the room
bed yawning
empty, orphaned

too smooth
for comfort.
Home truth dawning
slaps home:
Waiting lover
spirit footsteps
ear echoes
sounding,
resounding.

Oh, dear!

Coupling

Limbs link
    Linkages
        Weavers two
            Twisted
                Union of limbs
                      Affinity of bodies
                        Vibes
                Vibrations
            Tremors
        Separations
Air or detachment
Dynamite
    Of thrusts
        Perspiration
            Soaking wet
                Cool off
                Body motion freezes
                      Tranquil
                        Takes stock

Endless love

We two together
In our Disney world
Admit no prowler
We must have our
Belly laugh
Cauldron mix

Our witches' haunt then
Let's repossess
Do you really feel
Bewitched?
No witch-hunting there
Who would have thought it?
'Amosu!' the cry. She's a witch
When love is all I ask
And is what I believe I got
Now its tang lingers
Fire burning deep, searing
Brand me like your favoured pet
Where wouldn't I follow you?
Or lead, if you choose
Oh, but to waltz into a future
Configured to our taste
Always to be renewed by our love
Absence of pain, presence of praise
Flowers and gardens
Roses blooming for us
Red roses our favourite

Mother & child

(For nwanneka ezeokwuora justin)

Neither depth
Nor height
Can separate a mother
From her child

Her love is deep like a well
Her care a lifetime agenda
Nothing to do with gender
Male is to her what female is
Her feelings know no garths
She has the strength of a garrison
When called upon to defend her own
Reward comes in deep satisfaction
When even a tot displays appreciation
Of a mother's burning affection
Love
Trust
Intimacy
Close relationship
All there is when mother
And her baby gaze
Deep into each other's eyes

Random Songs

Unresolved questions

You ask: why do some leaves survive
      in winter and others don't?

I ask: why do some people love
      so well and others can't?

Since you refuse to give an answer
      to my question

I will give no answer
      to yours.

What went wrong?

Nothing is as ugly as dead friendship
Not even divorce could be so traumatic
Once there were two friends
Inseparable like Siamese twins
Until a bug bit one and infected the other

Friendship should not start in the first place
Only to be blighted at some point along the way
Scourge of heartache and bellyache
Recrimination does the soul no good
Bitterness for sure dries the bones
What went wrong? This sour after taste
Ruins appetite for new ventures;
galls the mind

Tell me, did you lose anything?
I know I lost something deep inside me.

---

* (In December, 2006, the bodies of five murdered prostitutes were
discovered around Ipswich in the UK within a space of ten days, sparking
fears that a serial killer–in the tradition of the infamous Jack the Ripper
in the 19th century and the Yorkshire Ripper twenty-five years ago–was
on the loose.)

Mad pursuit

Glory to God for the young
Life hangs heavy like a bunch of bananas
On those bent with age.
Youth is a sprightly thing, beckoning
Gets you on the move
To outrun an assailant
To outstrip a madman
On a stabbing spree
To stop a manicure of cure

Here he comes
His mind mixed-up, hallucination depot
Caught you pants down
In your room
Time to dialogue with your feet
Competing with wind
Madman inches behind

Flight ends after chase recedes
Blessings on your feet,
Losses count for nothing
Your bunch of keys the only casualty
After a mad chase
Without provocation

Ripper-style serial killer*

Lonely nights
in watery sepulchers
dregs of society:
the bodies of
five prostitutes
blight brooks
wallow in woodland
Hapless victims of
a serial killer?

Death unexplained
birds of night
glow worms
glittering
in the red-light area
of Ipswich
commercial sex workers–
hallowed by unholy
profession

O Daughters of Eve
fallen and fallen again
in the eye of disgrace,
it was siad you had wonderful
beginning, went to college
what then was your problem?
Who then is to blame
for your negative fame?
derailed by drug
lulled by lust

goaded by greed
ripped apart by a Ripper
on the loose

Is this a note of warning
to all who are whoring

---

*   In December, 2006, the bodies of five murdered prostitutes were discovered
around Ipswich in the UK within a space of ten days, sparking fears that a
serial killer–in the tradition of the infamous Jack the Ripper in the 19th
century and the Yorkshire Ripper twenty-five years ago–was on the loose.

Strange encounter

Bayreuth 2005. Dusk!
Glued to metal seat
Location: a bus-stop in the city's belly
I watch a drunk stagger towards me
Clutching a bottle
Wielding it like a gun
Belly heat, heart palpitation
Alone I quake: I feel truly trapped
Anxious, willing him to pass
Eyes shut tight. 'I'm an ant,' I imagine
Like I used to do back home
As a child, to escape terror
Pursued by demons spawned by malaria fever
Age of innocence's gone; illusion dead
Slain by hard facts of life–
Many like you have been attacked–
Self-delusion contemplating childish folly
Eyes fly open, fear becomes my heart
I watch! I wait!
Progress impeded by swigs taken with a leer
Drowning himself with fiery drink
Should I rise and run?–
The language of the cowardly
Is he blinded by the colourless sea
Of alcohol flooding his senses
Like a burst dam in the season of rain?

Oh the drumbeat that was my heart
His snake aura petrifies my rat reflex
I hug my seat, buttocks frozen
My gaze holds his, his mine

Each captive to the other
A seemingly endless game

Then an explosion: only a belch!
Spray of breath full of mist
Emptying into winter's cold visage
A longing dominate my senses,
Invisibility, like H.G. Well's hero:
The Invisible Man!
The bottle rises,
A potent weapon?
The threat ends at his swollen lips
Sucking noise, deep drinking, smacking sound
I recoil, wondering if he's been in a fight,
Waiting for an act, fair or foul
What an apparition!
  Crumpled clothes.
  Smelly.
  Frayed.
  Full of stains.
I hold my breath. Expecting what?
My eyes kill his.
Lurching to the right and to the left
He staggers past
My chest heaves, awash with relief
Exhales misty air,
In the distance, my bus hurtles towards me

Healthy eating–catch them young*

Nutritionist to kiddies–solemnly oracular–
'eat food rich in fibre
a portion of vegetables,
as many fruits as you can find
go natural
play safe
by eating right
tell Mum this is what you need'
vigorous campaign, big smiles
elaborate gestures to boot
maximum dosage of ego booster
print and electronic media agog with message
then comes Judgment Day–the test–
how much of this teaching
how many kids have imbibed–
31 October, to be precise
on Hallowe'en, formerly the day to celebrate
witches and wizards, in the UK
also eve of All Saints' Day
not to be caught napping
crusader tons of apples amass–
not the Edenic show for sure–
to give away to kiddies
in the spirit of *trick-or-treaters*
metropolis rattle with kiddies' patter
parading streets, knocking on doors
Ms. Nutritionist aglow with elation
cartons of enticing apples displays
to sharp and eager eyes
oh what a gaze it is!
ouch! Flabbergasted she is!

kiddies kick her door, retreating
all smiles wiped off furious faces
expectations expire in fumes of dislike
the devil take your apples!
away with them!–they seem to cry
one hundred kiddies that knock on her door
turning their noses up at the apples and bananas
children screaming for chocolates
salivating for sweet
　　　disaster!
Calamitous loss!
Madam Nutritionist
two hundred apples richer
gorged on two hundred bananas
crowned monarch of
fruit kingdom–FK
campaign gone awry
bleary eyes red from weeping
mourning failure
To bring healthy eating
To kiddies in the UK!

---

* In October 2006, many people in the UK, especially nutritionists and health workers cried out, because of the increase in the number of obese children. The campaign to educate young people and parents on the importance of healthy eating increased in tempo. But would children cooperate? They love their sweets and chocolates and pastry.

Lagos slums

Lagos teems
With numberless slums
most as old as the city

but new ghettoes form
at unparalleled pace
overcrowded hovels
cardboard contraptions
in some cases
houses on stilts
like stilt dancers
tottering at uncanny angles
dike tiwuo onyinyo–apparitions
dividing and sub-dividing
like amoeba
amoebic

streets exist
with solid structures
but plagued by
people-congestion
suffering from
humidity thralldom
and power cuts
blocked drains
singing mosquitoes
making music
night and day

no dull moment
overflowing
human traffic

action unlimited
homes double as shops
marketplaces pervasive
straggling street traders
money doublers
boasting to create wealth
for their clientele
themselves ash-mouthed
paupers. Dry buttocks

this earthly Hell
hole in the city
hides beauties
able to challenge
an Igbani Darego
daughters dreaming
of a Prince Charming
swooping down
to pull them out
of captivity
wiser ones, though
work their way
more permanent prize
their aspiration craves
education to acquire
passport to the good life
in foreseeable future

and to brighter zones
move
thus, beating the ghetto

Brave stab

1. News in Brief–
   Official news, of course –
   Observation confirmed
   Female presence
   On the increase
   In the vicinity
   Of
   Government House
   And
   Legislators' quarters
   And
   Near the Upper
   And Lower Houses

   Strange.

   Growing concern
   Security measures
   To be taken
   To prevent continued
   Trespass.

   Incidence of idleness
   On
   The part of
   Young women
   Frowned upon

   Hanging around
   Must be
   Discouraged

Governors
And
And Members of
House of Reps
Condemn this
Attitude in
Our women.'

2. News Behind The Scene –
   Unofficial news, of course –

   Some skeptics
   Regard it as rumour:

   'Politicians womanize
   Too much.
   Too many
   Women
   Around them

   Senators
   House of Reps members
   Culpable
   Shame!

   Distraction
   Must be put
   To an end.

   These men permanently
   Stand for erection
   Rather than election
   The nation must
   Call then to
   Attention!

Sex scandal
Must cease

It is said
They get migraine
If they *see*
Same woman two times

They change them
As actresses
Change dresses
From one seductress
To another
Walking the street

Sex pushed
High up
The agenda
In place of
National agenda.

They bedhop from
Betty to Belinda
Halima to Harriet
Ebele to Enitan.
Slaves to
Passion
&
Pleasure

What time
Do they have to
Steer the ship of state
Before it stalls

Or sinks
They
Deport dubious lovers
Import impressionable ones

If press sniffs fresh scandal
It is silenced
With threats
Or short-gun

3. Reports conflicting:
   Where does truth
   Begin and end?

   The long
   And
   The short
   Of it is:
   Judge for yourself.

Final journey

'I got a train to catch
London Waterloo
got me return ticket
see you later, love.'

Statement routine
long kiss
on mouth
clinging embrace
affirmation of trust
confidence exchange
one lover to another
the waiting
begins...

He never made it back.
not now
never will.

December!
Month of greed
great expectations
pressure on pockets
crime infested
climate of fear
palpable...

Enter the Terminator!
Life terminated
extermination
midstream.

Knifed!
In street corner.

Reason?
Purloin a purse
gleaned earlier
during recce –
military parlance
reconnaissance.

Brotherhood
of thieves
another victim
end of the road,
road in bloom
potential skewered
bliss blistered
hope hacked.

Victim: No. What?
Does it matter?
Vital statistics:
plus one!
Numbers swell.

Bewilderment
a great cloud
hanging over
the beloved.

Tone of silence

Scented garden
    of the mind.
Musings
    in dreamland.
Faraway
    prying eyes evade.
Living presences
    in hiding.
Tuneful moment
    bursting melody.
In the song of a songbird
    subsumed.
O Man! Woman!
    get thee behind me.
Vision soars
    hour of immanence.
The quiet pull
    pool immersion.
Watery presence
    life rejuvenate.
I die in you
    you in me.
Time, ample time
    for resurrection.
A rebirth
    New beginning.
Echo of life
    muffled.
Enchanted
    I linger.
Listening to
    soothing tone of silence

When all i see are strangers

Flight from the known
To the unknown
Alone in a crowd
Around me their chatter
Raucous laughter. Timbre robust.
Market voices, in city-scape
In multiple tongues
None identical to mine
I am deaf and dumb

In a place I'm not understood
Or appreciated
How will they know that I'm friendly –
That I'm somebody:
Mba ama onye ukwu
If they do not talk to me
Or listen to me talk to them?
Secret glances pregnant with meaning
Bloated with calculation
Barbed wire words
Tear the flesh of air
Impale motion, whip up emotion
Are they talking about me?
'If you hear catch am, run!'
Madman in my village always says
But I cannot tell a word from another
General babble, puncture in air tubes
Is that Chinese? Sounds Japanese?
In motley garb, lurid in colour, texture
If I speak, will they think I'm child-like?
Or consider it a jabber? Gabble?
So theirs sounds

Stutter. *Numkwam!**
A drag, a string of incomprehensible jargon

Morning rush hour
Flights of trains
Express heading for who-knows-where
Train load of commuters
South West Trains, London Waterloo bound
Inter-city coaches, well-trodden pedestrian crossings
Always I'm sole raven
Surrounded by egrets
Perhaps few Japs or Chinks
Sometimes Pakis or Injuns
Mostly ravens do not fly across this domain
Few indeed; egret suburb pure and simple
Except, of course, for occasional hybrids
Button nose, straight face. Superior!
Improved pedigree. Luminous of skin!
Mid-zone between ravendom and egretdom
Distance keep; contamination not allowed!

Heart tumbles, frog jump. Ravens sighted
You glow. Eager gestures of affection
Our raven-skin betrays us
Makes us stick out like a sore thumb
We who left our lake of fire
For the glitter of frozen lands
Each face I invoke; seeking eye contact
Head averted. Gaze anywhere
But where it should be
That air of indifference. Nonchalance
Lack of recognition. Lost identity
Beast of no nation. Nation of beasts
Damn you for selling your identity
For a mess of porridge

Labour merchant
Expert in Dirty Jobs:
Security Guard. Chamber Maid. Factory Hand
Cleaning others' filth for a low fee
Each visage I scan. Searching for nationality
Not tattooed on skin; more of speculation
Kenyan? Angolan? Tanzanian? Chadian?
Or Nigerian? Ghanaian? Senegalese?
Or any abandoned *other*?
Which category claims you?
Seasoned or seasonal deserter?
Reasoned desertion?
Which propelled movement? Who knows?
Expediency dictates
The tune of every desertion
Every guided or misguided migration

(* nonsense)

Woman being

Dem sabi wahala
Tiger de sleep
Trouble go carry am for tail
Na wahala be dat
WoMan palava
WoeMan palaver
Masculine gender strong
Feminine agenda cunny pass

The choice na your own
How-so-ever you be named
Mankind versus Womankind
Kingdom or Queendom
Abi History na Herstory
Son of de soil
Daughter of de domain
Woe to man forever or
Woo man forever
Dem say complementarity
Better pass superiority
Parity or Equality
Dem two good-o
Nwoke and *Nwanyi*
Okunri and *Obirin*
Megida and *Worigida*
Embrace dis philosophy
Choose life and live
Choose war and wane
Court man and be womanized
Count on man and be unmanned
Disregard man, you dey 'high and dry'
Na 'no win' situation
Eternal game of Woman being!

After the harvest

Bare fields
After the harvest
Silos burst with grains
Crammed to the brim
Tubers swell the ban
Banning hunger

Sky translucent
Weeping days are over
Rain long dissolved in the sun
Waiting for next season
Clouds disperse
Searching for height
A new hiding place

Where are your indigo shrouds
That recently draped the sky?

Moonlight sweeps the arena
Blinking stars set the stage
For vigorous night serenade
Here a lover itches to lay his hands
On the beloved. There a maiden sits
Coyly, hands folded between knees
Clusters of children, impatient
For play or story to begin, fidget
Cropped heads bob:
Up and down, up and down
Like canaries singing in cages
Men bent with age take their seats
Cast liquid eyes around, as mouths gush
Re-telling old tales of their youth

Recalling past triumphs
Women hug babies sucking
Gum-imprisoned breasts
Their men virile, gazing at their
Offspring, planning for more

Chaa gbii! Stories fall into hungry ears
Hypnotized.
Eerie silence bonds listeners
Like a mother, the moon watches, smiles

Enticing termites

Mama's motions
shadow looms
bends double
over comatose forms
a shake
gentle at first
solicitous
then near violent
branding shake
blinding tug
marked hunters
startled scramble
on wobbly legs
sleepy-eyed stretch
yawns
termite night
harvest time.

Sack in hand
trooping out
a troop of four
two stragglers
dragging feet
torches bright
palm fibre-made
perfect ferret.

A cove in anthill-side
chanced upon
termitedom.
pseudo-earthquake

silent quake
gyrating termites
wings a-quiver
more gyrations
million-strength
awesome
renouncing wings
some wingless
rapidly coupling
tail-to-tail mating
their bliss halting,
we scooped them
into yawning sack
soon astir
with termite lives.

Torches burning merrily
our hearts aglow
Nko, Nna, Nonye and me–
happy hunters,
our eyes
feasting
on a feast
sweetest
in anticipation.

Memorial Songs

Voice of night masquerade

(In memory of ezenwa-ohaeto)

1. a cry in the night
   night masquerade
   oke mmonwu
   dreaded mask!

2. voice of ancestors
   revered emissary
   venerated spirit
    spirit encounter

3. coordination in
   elocution
   medley of sounds
   cacophony

4. voice tremor
   Ogbaagu's timbre
   Steeped in mystery
   Cultic

5. Monkey-spirit
   in attendance
   cried all night
   time prejudged

6. announced
   transition
   premature
   Night garnished with sorrow

7. the night old

the crier young
word weaver
fledgling

8. release
   there in the *obi*
   of Spirit King
   masks assemble

9. voices break
   drowned by silence
   rise
   fall

10. ebbing, flowing
    strained ears
    tingle
    tangled voices

11. meaning not discerned
    message not interpreted
    mmonwu anaa!
    beyond the abyss

12. big masks depart
    small masks flood field
    fall into pit
    ignorant of pitfall

13. permission to fall out?
    Flight to motherland
    in the midst
    of mixed dances

14. farting in air
    mystery for fly
    prized soul
    a price to pay

15. a price
    on your head
    for untimely push
    into oblivion

16. sans prognosis?
    Cold comfort–
    migration mourned
    in multiple climes

17. Songbird, adieu!
    Laa n'udo, Gaa nkeoma
    go sing in brighter
    spheres

Death of a princess

1. Like a meteor
   From outer space
   Diana, Princess of Wales
   Jetted into world space

   Luminous
   Incandescent

   World waved
   Stronger she waxed
   Dazzling light

   Waning soon
   Brief flare
   Snuffed out in
   The Pont de l'Alma
   Tunnel, in Paris

   August in carriage
   Died August, 1997

2. Outrage. Rage
   World mourned
   Still mourning
   Ten years after

   Enemy within
   Enemy without
   Culpable
   Speculation rife
   Paparazzi pursuit
   Then smash

Failed relationship
Her bane?
New relationship
Riled Royalty

MI6 prowled
As Diana & Dodi
In Paris roved
Conspiracy or
Coincidence?

3. Royalty indicted?
Exonerated by
Lord Steven Report

But lord of Harrods,
Fayed, temper frayed
Venomous
Cried foul
Royal murder
Diana & Dodi victims

4. Evidence?–
Flash of light
Car tampering
Spy plot
Camilla plot
Fear of engagement
Diana herself feared
Her fate sealed
To be 'chopped'
Like Mary
Queen of Scots

5. Conclusion discordant:
   'tragic accident'–
   official claim
   'brutal murder'–
   unofficial claim

6. Final word:
   Diana is dead
   Rest is hers in death

   Forever free from
   Prying paparazzi

   Matchless like
   Her Greek namesake
   Only lacking immortality

   Farewell Princess
   Your works live
   Living memorial of
   Your fruitful life

Farewell, great patriarch

The bitterest news of the season
Dealt us a crippling blow
Ears tingled, eyes blurred
He who sat astride the threshold took a flying jump
Over the gulf to regain his former home
Where ancestors grown impatient waited
To receive a pilgrim homeward bound

Who then is left to guide the young ones?
These days that witness a world turned upside down
When to reflect is but to set the brain on fire
The body quakes like extinct Vesuvius
Like active Kilimanjaro

Who will answer our questions?
Who spell out our genealogy?
And recall even the most obscure ancestor?
Ezeukwu's exploits recount?
Who will trace for us that ever-growing family tree
Of the children of Onugo and Otuonahu?

If you see the strong-hearted one, greet him
Greet also the rest of the clan
And those who lately joined the band
A branch has withered, fallen
Surely, others will spring up, strong and graceful?

Worthy son of our forebear
May the ancestors receive you with pomp'
May you arrive early, as dew drips
From the tree of life to bathe your hot face
You have run your race like a stallion

Your maker to view with new eyes
Which see beyond the confine of faith
What if we still need you
On this side of the great divide?
What is the seeker in me cries against this loss?
What does it matter?
You are in a better place
Sleep on, in the abode of light
Where to be is to be in bliss
Resting in the bosom of your Master

Farewell, valiant soul!
Komesia,* great historian
And guardian of the word

You were a storehouse of knowledge
You taught us about love and unity
You paved the way for peace
Freedom choirmaster
We will not forget your legacy of carWe who are left to mourn you.

* Adieu! We will meet again!

Muritala mohammed

1. Longest-lived
   head of state
   in mind's cocoon
   fondest at heart
   multi-purposed
   single-minded
   leader approved
   though by barrel
   of gun enthroned
   winsome winner
   race so fast
   sharp corners
   death-trap
   you artless
   trusting
   behold wolves
   in sheep's clothing
   forever revered
   is brevity
   the secret?

2. Crux of the matter:
   not how long
   but how well
   power utilized
   for common good
   your challenge
   none so far
   tackled
   your standard
   none matched
   how then could
   thoughts of
   superceding you
   ever arise?

Bola ige

Ever seen such
audacity?
leopard
caught in his den
by beasts
daft of mind
brainless
except to shed
blood

Times of terror
tumble upon us
time seizure
angst angled

Thunderbolt
in home front
not marketplace

Bullets pelted
pumped with glee
bullet-riddled
one body
had bullets for three

Fear swallowed
public voice
profit pocketed
cornered conscience

Gifted drummers

drummed the crime
to whip up ire
but no dancing
feet stormed
the empty stage

But, whose name was
the throbbing
sound blaring?

Lest we forget
the lawgiver
interpreter of law
writer
art lover
culture connoisseur
once ruler
of the West
prominent politician

It was he
the drums
pulsated his name

His blood still cries
for justice

Will he get it?

Time will tell.

At home everywhere
(For nina emma mba)

O woman of substance
Woman of straw
Crossing seas, rivers
Oceans with wide girths
Following your true love
Joined once, constant
You remained; love of a lifetime
My fair sister from far Australia
Fairer in heart than even in skin
Service more than skin-deep
You were willing to render
Nwanne di na Mba
You taught us to be proud
Of our heritage, our identity

Wherever your spirit reclines
Or roves to conquer more territories
I know your brilliant mind
Lights up dark glades
For death has no hold over you

At home with history
In love with literature
In each a niche you carved out
And shone like diamond
Nwayi oma, nodu nkeoma
Well the battle fought
Now it's night
But round the corner is light

Songs For Women

Violated ogoni women

Sisters, sisters, sisters
three times I call you
tears flow down
as blood flows
Delta not lacking
these bizarre
tributaries
one red like your soil
the other
colourless
like your life
savaged first
you watch
your daughters
ravaged
by men armed
to the teeth
some younger than you:
men of blood
on a blood-drinking
spree. Virgins' hymen
torn to shreds
with violence
impunity!
their blood
mingles
with the blood and soil
of the land

Sisters, wipe your tears
Many before you
This path have walked –

Biafra remote arena
Rwanda only yesterday
your voices
in court of conscience–
Oputa Panel
ring, ring again
will anything come out of it?
another white paper?
swelling the volume
of previous ones
while the volume
of your voice rises
strident
announcing in public
what our culture
classifies
as taboo
no female wants to admit
a rape victim she
the stigma
oh, the branding!
smear of shame
indelible
yet, courage fails you not
resolute
you scream it: RAPE!
let all ears that hear it
tingle. Burst with pain

Leona launched

(A new star in the british music scene is born)

1.

Big take
Of X Factor Crown
Lioness-hearted Leona
Aged twenty-one
Your dawn
Dawning bright
Singing Angel
Going solo
Bursting out
With
'A Moment Like This'

2.
Hybrid child
British born
London bred
White mother
Black father
Straddling two cultures
Best of two worlds
At home in both

3.
Fortuned favoured
Crowned champion
First woman to win
The show
Or reach the final

Your hit topping the chart

Receptionist turned
Millionaire overnight
A million pound record deal

The world at your feet
Sky within reach
You dreamed
Your dream paid off
Sweat, tears, hard work
Determination
Watered this victory

Savour it
Nectar excreted
By your melodious voice.

Ode to the successful woman writer

Dogged, undaunted, goal-oriented, obsessive-driven woman!
Burning with vision and the desire to change things
It was a great day when you emerged
From the wings and occupied the centre stage
In full visibility, refusing to be observer or spectator
You stormed the stage, away from the back door of history
My sister, listen, always stay where the action is
You liberated the word to become its utterer and proclaimer
You no longer mutter or stutter
Your inferiority complex evaporated like mist
You are no longer one of the crowd, but first among equals
Queen of Letters: that is your name
You beat the drum and others dance
You leaped high and reached the top
To shatter the glass ceiling
With your fists you shattered it
Like a battering ram.

To a grieving mother

Loss too great
For contemplation
Oh, the mystery of it
Premature departure

A year after
Raw still
Your pain

Pain steals your joy
Wound raw
Like a spear thrust
In the heart
Hammer blow
Stunned
Will this pain never cease?
Void so deep–
The feel
What can fill?

Remember!
Pining not your portion
Depression fight
Not by suppression
But full acceptance
Divine intervention
Blessed assurance

Hope hopping
Into your heart
Radiating in your home
Sorrow stifled

Annihilated
Your sadness
Turn into gladness

Weep no more
Let joy take root
Service feed
Roots of joy

Sister, it's time
To repossess
Your joy and move on!

Women of my land

How may I sing of you?
Your so-called beauty
of 'the black woman' fame?
Shall I sing of your skin
dark as midnight
light as ochre?

I'd rather sing
your wet eyes weeping
over your dying children
your callused hands
deep in dirty water
buried in soil
nurture your goal
belly big with child
re-populate communities
disease decimated
war walloped
your slaving rewarded
with enslavement

I will sing your endurance
even in the teeth of terror
tyranny defeated
with thunder of patience

Sister, time ripe
like lion roar
your thunder turn
patience to impatience
ignite the soaking wood
with passion fumes
long suppressed

Dress to kill

Over the centuries
You dressed to kill
    In a way
    Your way

Naked you roamed
Jigida, circle of beauty
    Your skin aglow:
    As if fully-clothed

Then your innocence was your armour
Skin was cloth
    But times changed
    And ushered in batik–*ekwerike*

Like one with ears: falling
In line, in love:
    Skirt billowed
    Tight bodice

Trouser-clad
Walking tight rope
    Lappa–gift-wrap
    Wrapped round your figure

Like *aniga*
You bloomed, dressed to kill
    Eyes awash
    New fashions to conquer.

But today marks your return
To anachronistic nudity
    See how you are booed
    Age of innocence lost for ever

Kraftgriots

Also in the series (POETRY) continued

Joe Ushie: *A Reign of Locusts* (2004)
Paulina Mabajoye: *The Colours of Sunset* (2004)
Segun Adekoya: *Guinea Bites and Sahel Blues* (2004)
Ebi Yeibo: *Maiden Lines* (2004)
Barine Ngaage: *Rhythms of Crisis* (2004)
Funso Aiyejina: *I,The Supreme & Other Poems* (2004)
'Lere Oladitan: *Boolekaja: Lagos Poems 1* (2005)
Seyi Adigun: *Bard on the Shore* (2005)
Famous Dakolo: *A Letter to Flora* (2005)
Olawale Durojaiye: *An African Night* (2005)
G. 'Ebinyo Ogbowei: *let the honey run & other poems* (2005)
Joe Ushie: *Popular Stand & Other Poems* (2005)
Gbemisola Adeoti: *Naked Soles* (2005)
Aj. Dagga Tolar: *This Country is not a Poem* (2005)
Tunde Adeniran: *Labyrinthine Ways* (2006)
Sophia Obi: *Tears in a Basket* (2006)
Tonyo Biriabebe: *Undercurrents* (2006)
Ademola O. Dasylva: *Songs of Odamolugbe* (2006), winner, 2006 ANA/Cadbury
    poetry prize.
George Ehusani: *Flames of Truth* (2006)
Abubakar Gimba: *This Land of Ours* (2006)
G. 'Ebinyo Ogbowei: *the heedless ballot box* (2006)
Hyginus Ekwuazi: *Love Apart* (2006), winner 2007 ANA/Cadbury poetry prize &
    winner, 2007 ANA/NDDC Gabriel Okara poetry prize.
Abubakar Gimba: *Inner Rumblings* (2006)
Albert Otto: *Letters from the Earth* (2007)
Aj. Dagga Tolar: *Darkwaters Drunkard* (2007)
Musa Idris Okpanachi: *The Eaters of the Living* (2007), winner, 2008 ANA/Cadbury
    poetry prize
Tubal Cain: *Mystery in our Stream* (2007), winner 2006 ANA/NDDC Gabriel
    Okara poetry prize
Sola Owonibi: *Chants to the Ancestors* (2007)
John Iwuh: *Ashes and Daydreams* (2007)
Adewale Aderinale: *The Authentic* (2007)
Sola Owonibi: *Chants to the Ancestors* (2007)
Ebi Yeibo: *The Forbidden Tongue* (2008)
Doutimi Kpakiama: *Salute to our Mangrove Giants* (2008)
Halima M. Usman: *Spellbound* (2008)
Gregory Osaji Odiakosa *Raindrops on Roses* (2008)
Hyginus Ekwuazi: *Dawn into Moonlight: All Around Me Dawning* (2008), winner
    2008 ANA/NDDC Gabriel Okara poetry prize
Ismaila Bala Garba & Abdullahi Ismaila (eds.): *Pyramids: An Anthology of Poems
    from Northern Nigeria* (2008)

133

Denja Abdullahi: *Abuja Nunyi (This is Abuja)* (2008)
Japhet Adeneye: *Poems for Teenagers* (2008)
Seyi Hodonu: *A Tale of Two in Time (Letters to Susan)* (2008)
Ibukun Babarinde: *Running Splash of Rust and Gold* (2008)